The Hours
In Between

P.Bodi

P. Bodi

You have survived every
Day that has passed,
Every day that you were
Convinced would be your last,
Be proud of staying and for
Seeing it through, because
Recovery, hope, healing is in you.

The Hours In Between

Think of 'eventually',
Think of the day you will
Look back and find
Yourself grateful,

Grateful that you
Stayed, that you grew,
Grateful that you did
It all for you.

P.Bodi

You are enough in what you've
Done and who you have become,
Who you've been in the past and
Who you are in this moment,

We are all stepping more into
Ourselves everyday, learning
We are worthy as we are and
In how we are growing.

The Hours In Between

Your life matters,
It does, from the
First moment
That it began,

We wake up to the
World unsure and
Afraid, it's a profound
Sort of magic, deciding
For ourselves to live,
To stay.

Yes, your life matters.
You—with fears and dreams, challenges and successes, hopelessness and hope. And hope may be in short supply right now. But feelings are not always to be believed. It is a profound sort of magic, choosing to meet tomorrow. Deciding to wake up into a day as unsure as your first. Living is not so simple an endeavour, and in the face of it all, here you are. That takes tremendous strength. You matter, and I think you'll come to see it too. If only for a while, let me hold hope for you.

The Hours In Between

Believe in the space you've yet to fill,
In the light that you've yet to see,
There is more of life to be felt,
There is more of you to be.

P.Bodi

Seeking the life you want
To live is not selfish, it is
A gift to others as well
As to you—

To show others they
Have permission to dream,
To hope, to find what
They are truly
Meant to do.

Relapse is often a part
Of the process of becoming well,
It doesn't have to be the end,

Sometimes, we have to
Begin again and again.

P.Bodi

Be real, honest, true,
The world needs you
To be you.

The Hours In Between

In us is grown a change
That we speak into the world,
All heralds of a future we
Can make bright, we
Can make a little
More whole,

Hope is something we
All can come to hold.

P.Bodi

You are a herald, bright, of a future and of a hope to be shared. You, with your gifts and in your unique light can make the world more whole, even when that doesn't feel true. We all carry with us those things only we can do, only what we can be, only what we can bring to this life. Seek connection, seek warmth, seek empathy for yourself and others. Brilliant warmth, light, purpose, is all found in you.

The Hours In Between

You are a gift,
You would be missed,
Stay here now for yourself
And remember that there
Are others who would
Feel your absence,

The effect you have on
This world is lasting.

P.Bodi

Find the little things to keep
You going, those small
Lights to tend to, to
Grow, to keep you warm
In their steady glow.

The Hours In Between

You decide what's worth
Your time, effort, and heart,

Remember there is always
A place for you in this world
To take part.

There has always been a place for you here. There is home to be found, people to love and to love you in return, purpose to be discovered and nurtured. You decide your path, what you want to do with the time you have been given. You are needed in this world; your gifts and warmth are needed.

The Hours In Between

Treasure the love you have,
Accept that warmth and
Keep it close,

And remember that you
Are deserving of both
Being loved as you are,
As well as loved in
Your capacity
For inner growth.

Look at you,
Still here,
Reaching out
To what light
There is to
Be found,

No matter how dark,
There is a brightness
To be held—yours,
Stunning, profound.

The Hours In Between

You are capable beyond what you may
Believe, you are enough as you are
And have always been, your strength
Is built in every moment that you
Choose to keep going, here you are
At the center of it all, blooming,
Only ever growing.

We deserve to be surrounded by
Those who will treat us right,
With trust, and with respect,

And we must grow the
Self-love to decide what
We will and will not accept.

The Hours In Between

Believe what may feel
Unbelievable in this moment:
Believe you are valuable and
Worthy, because it's true,

Don't let yourself
Wish you were
Anyone but you.

Wishing I was someone else was a disservice to myself. To what only I can be, to what only I can do, to what only I can give to this world.

You are a gift. You are worthy and valuable as yourself. Let go of trying to be someone else and become more of you. This life is only yours to live, so live it honestly.

The Hours In Between

We face endless trials in life,
One thing after another without
Rest or reprieve, unsure if we
Can make it through to what
Will come next,

But you've survived your
Hardest days if you're here
Now, and the most we can
Ask of ourselves is to take
It all step by step,

You are resilient, you are
Strong, and you've been
Ready all along.

P.Bodi

Getting better does not look one way,
Does not feel the same for everyone,
Does not take a set amount of time—
We are individuals, and healing is
Not a task, but a process,

Comparison does not help
Anyone to get where they
Need to be, we are all
Different in how we
Make progress.

The Hours In Between

If you're asking yourself if you are
'Good enough', 'worthy enough',
Or simply 'enough' at all, it's likely
The answer will be 'never enough';
This is a dead-end we are drawn
Back to in the hope it will bring
Us some sort of self-love,

But the truth is, you are worthy
Exactly where you are right now,
There's no need to question—
You are enough, and you
Deserve your own
Acceptance.

P.Bodi

Maybe you feel you've lost
What it means to be you,
What you value, what is true,
Maybe you feel confused,

But as long as you have yourself—
The person you want to be,
The life you want to live
Can still be found,

You deserve to be you,
Your purpose is profound.

The Hours In Between

You can be the voice of
Kindness others need to hear,
You can be of comfort, you
Can speak from a place of love,

And be kind to you,
This you have always
Been worthy of.

We are that which loves, and that which is loved. You have warmth to share with others, and warmth to receive. We can learn to operate from a source of love instead of from shame or fear. We can gift comfort and kindness to others, the way we have always deserved and needed this kindness ourselves. You have always been worthy of this.

You can touch the lives
Of others, you can bring
Warmth to what is cold,
Kindness to that which hurts,

And it starts with taking
Care of yourself first.

Maybe you don't know yourself well,
Almost like a stranger,
But there is always time to discover,
To explore and to become,
This growth is never done.

The Hours In Between

There is meaning
To be made, to be
Felt and to be lived,

There are things only
Your talents can give.

P.Bodi

Sometimes it has to start small,
Recovery begins with one step—
Deciding to try for yourself,

You are worth your own support,
And you deserve others help.

The Hours In Between

Hope can be a fickle thing,
Hard to hold and keep and believe,
Sunk inside the feeling that
You'll never find relief,

And feelings are hard to
Question when they're so
Convincing and loud,

But hopelessness is not
A prophet, hope can
Always be found.

Hopelessness is no prophet. It cannot tell your future, even when it is convincing, even when it is loud, even when it feels undeniable. Maybe you have been without hope for some time, maybe hopelessness is all you know. It still is no guarantee you'll always feel this way. Hold the hope that hope will arrive. There is more life to be lived, and there is more of you to discover and grow.

The Hours In Between

Your pain is real,
And maybe right now,
It's all you're able to feel,

But recovery is real too,
You've always had
It in you to heal,
That's always
Been found
In you.

P.Bodi

Question fear,
And hold onto the
Hope that hope has
Been waiting for you
All along,

If you've yet to feel it,
Give your hope time,
Just as the night waits
Patient for the dawn.

The Hours In Between

Sometimes we aren't thriving—
Simply doing the best we can,
Trying, learning, surviving,

And here you are now,
Here you are alive,
Be grateful to yourself
For choosing to stay,
For choosing to fight
For this life.

The flowers do not ask if they
Are good enough to bask in
The sun's warmth, to receive
The light they need to thrive,

Maybe we can learn something
In their 'simply being', that we
Don't need to ask ourselves if
We are enough, instead to accept
Day's steady glow as it arrives,
Soft petals as our guide.

The Hours In Between

Life is a series of endless changes,
People walk in and out of our lives,
Ways of being shift, we become,
We grow, we fall and we get
Back up, and sometimes we
Find ourselves stuck,

Even then, even when we feel
Things will never improve, we
Surprise ourselves with just
How much we can come to
Grow, that even here,
We can bloom.

We can surprise ourselves in this life when we do not fully believe in our strength and resilience. That you are still here despite the hard days you've lived, that is unwavering proof of your capacity to grow and to bloom. Change is never-ending, and so is your courage.

You are no small thing,
You are not meant to
Shrink yourself, you
Are meant to flourish
Into your own,

To take up space,
To reach and reach,
To let yourself grow.

P.Bodi

You deserve recovery,
Relief and rest,
Struggling could never
Make you less.

There is strength within you,
The kind that can be grown,
The kind you've had all along,

Facing your fears, your challenges,
That is what makes you strong.

The sun that lifts the
Flowers high, is a
Light that lives in
You, too,

Rise to the day's
Rhythm, as if the
Dawn is not a
Given, breathe
And be and
Bloom.

The Hours In Between

When faced with what
Seems the unsolvable
And the hopeless, we
Name ourselves weak,
Broken, a burden,

But that is exactly where strength
Blossoms—in our resilience, in
Our feeling-it-all, in our learning.

We often reserve harsh words to only ourselves. That we are weak, that we are broken, that we are a burden. When we feel hopeless and stuck, we may forget empathy and compassion for our struggle and for ourselves. But that you are here, that you have made it to today—that shows your strength and resilience. You are worth supporting in your hard moments, and there is hope for you. We can learn new coping skills and new ways to approach ourselves and the world. Let yourself feel what you are feeling with compassion and without shame, and give yourself kindness, empathy, and grace.

The Hours In Between

When reaching for what
You want at your best—
Find it in the voice that shakes,
The heart that hammers,
The breath unsteady and
Brilliantly alive, fear can tell
Us what matters to us most,
We can let it be our guide.

P.Bodi

Nourish the neglected,
Tend to your feelings,
Because they matter,
And you deserve to heal,

Acknowledge that which
Is hard to feel.

The Hours In Between

Take the shape of kindness,
Fold yourself into the warmth
You have denied,

It's always been in you,
That steady light to
Bring to life.

P.Bodi

Empathy is something you can give,
And something you can recieve,
A kindness shared for its own sake,
Feeling connected, together, seen.

The Hours In Between

Here we are, in
The in-between,
On the edge of
A world not one of
Us has seen,

We are all growing,
Take comfort in that
You are not alone,
Not in this, in this
Tomorrow not
Yet known.

P.Bodi

We all step forward as one into a world none of us yet know. We are together in this. We face change in our own unique ways, but you are not alone.

This is the in-between. It is the state of uncertainty, of anxiety and excitement the same; it is the inevitable tomorrow, the washing away of what has gone and the rising of what is arriving. Know that we do not know what can come, but take comfort in the knowledge that you are strong enough to face it.

The Hours In Between

The question of 'who
Has it worse' denies
The validity of your
Own true pain,

It covers your struggle
In even more shame,

Everyone that
Struggles is worth
Being helped, is
Worth being heard,

We all deserve to
Heal that which hurts.

P.Bodi

Imagine yourself looking back,
Grateful that you fought for you,
That you chose recovery, that
Despite it all, you grew,

This journey isn't easy,
It may be the hardest thing
You ever do, but it's always been
Worth it, you've always been worth
It, because recovery's in you.

The Hours In Between

Sometimes we hold onto
That which drags us down—
More committed to falling
Than to recovering,

But that is no promise you'll
Always feel the same way,

Believe in hope for tomorrow
If not for today.

The end of a relationship only
Brings you closer to the people
That truly care, and away from
Those who do not align,

Your light deserves to be shared,
To let yourself truly shine.

Give yourself the grace to grow,
Be patient, you are not to be rushed,
This living, this becoming, is a
Process we can learn to trust.

This is a process we can learn to trust. There is no time-limit on growth. There is not even a finish-line, or an end-point. Because this is a journey that never ends, and that is a wonderful thing. That we are never done, and that we are constantly becoming and adapting to change and developing more and more into the person we are meant to become. You cannot be rushed. Patience is not only necessary, but a gift you can give to yourself that is kind, that acknowledges your own pace, and that is compassionate when you feel you are not doing enough. You are enough. You are worthy where you are; whole, but never complete.

You are not a burden,
And you deserve those
Who value your presence,

You have always been worthy,
Never once 'less-than'.

P.Bodi

We all make mistakes,
That is a part of being a person,
Living a life is synonymous
With learning.

The Hours In Between

Here you are now,
Growing despite it all,
Blooming and reaching
As only you can,
Never were you
Meant to stay small.

There are things we hold onto,
Things that are no longer present,
Things longing and absent,
Focused not on what we
Have but what we haven't,

Circumstances, people,
Places, feelings, it's okay
To miss them, to want
Them back, this is part
Of healing.

The Hours In Between

Wherever you were taught
To pretend as a child, to act
As someone you were not,
To ignore your desires, your
Needs, and your feelings,

Give yourself the space, now,
To dedicate to you, to kindness,
And to your healing,

You have always mattered,
You have always been worthy
Of unconditional love and
Appreciation, let this moment
Be self-compassion's
Invitation.

Trust that you are lovable. Trust that you will find the kind of people that affirm that truth. Those who will give you space to be the most authentic version of yourself.

Until then, be the voice of kindness you have always needed and deserved. Let this moment be an invitation to be more forgiving and self-compassionate. You have always been worthy of that.

Every scar that clings
To you, the wounds
That we keep hidden,
Shame we can't
Bear to tell,

This deserves healing,
And you are not a burden,
You have always been
Worthy of others help.

It is true that pain is inevitable,
That it doesn't go away forever, that
It returns like an unwelcome guest,
And poses the question: 'Will I ever
Feel better?'

But hard moments are exactly where
Recovery is grown, that you're still
Trying holds the capacity for hope
And happiness to be known.

The Hours In Between

Be with what is here right now,
With what comes and then
Goes just the same,

Be with yourself in every way
That you are, release
Judgement, release shame.

What is a good life to you?
What brings fulfillment, purpose,
What makes you feel alive?

Reach and find and hold it close,
What it means for you to thrive.

The Hours In Between

Love is given to us,
And sometimes we don't
Know what to do,
We don't know how
To receive,

That we are unworthy
Of others warmth may have
Become a closely held belief,

Try and open up a little,
Like a flower turning slowly
To the sun, to live and believe—
Despite what you may feel, that
You are deserving of love.

Maybe you have been taught that love is a kindness reserved for others, never a kindness you were deserving of.

Maybe you have been loved honestly, in all that you are, and you still couldn't feel its warmth. Opening up is hard. As we grow alongside fear and pain, we close up in the desperate hope that we will never feel hurt again. But that which we thought would protect us only ends up perpetuating hurt.

Face those whose love for you is true, safe. Like a flower opening to the sun, let their light in, and let yourself breathe.
You deserve this warmth.

Our hurt can be addictive,
Self destruction a vice,
A familiar comfort,
A way to cope,

But we can step out of
The cycle, we can learn
To hope.

P.Bodi

We cannot decide what to feel,
Happiness is not a choice
To be made,

Even negative emotions
Have their place.

The Hours In Between

We get so caught up
In the trappings of
Pressure, of stress,

Of feeling like our
Worth is based on
Our achievements,
As if mistakes or
Imperfection could
Make us less,

But your worth has
Always been true,
In all that makes
You, you.

P.Bodi

There is a difference between
Giving up and resting,
Relapse and reprieve,
And even then, we can
Choose to get back up from
The worst we have felt,
Our most hopeless and distraught,

Choose to work through that
Which wants to keep you down,
Again and again, and one day,
You will be grateful that you fought.

The Hours In Between

You don't have to become
Brave, because you
Already are, keep
Growing as only
You can, that will
Take you far.

Courage looks like you. Being here now, despite it all, speaks of your innate strength. Be proud of staying. Be proud of committing to tomorrow. You are growing even through your fear. There has always been a place for you here.

Another's beauty says
Nothing about your own,
There is room for all of
Us to shine, to glow.

P.Bodi

We compare,
We compare and
We find ourselves
Wrong,

But you've been worthy,
You've been enough
All along,

Put to rest those
Thoughts that wish
To drag you down,

In comparison, your
Sense of true worth
Can never be found.

The Hours In Between

Honesty,
Authenticity,
To be loved at
Your most true,

This is the kind
Of love we all deserve,
The kind that accepts
You for you.

What star draws you forward,
What do you want for
Yourself at your brightest?

Listening to yourself, to
What you truly desire, that
Is a profound sort of kindness.

The Hours In Between

What courage it takes to
Be fully yourself, to reject
The masks you've worn
And the words you've
Claimed were your own,

To be unapologetic,
To be real in flaws and
In your strengths—
To be seen, to be
Heard, to truly
Be known.

Authenticity, being honestly you in front of yourself and others, can feel terrifying. We become afraid of judgement because it will hit harder and sharper when we are being true. But this is also how deep connection is built. This is where purpose and fulfillment are found. You deserve to be loved as yourself, to be truly known, to be valued in all the things that only you can do.

Maybe you feel somewhere
Lost in the middle,
Where the fight feels
Impossible to win,
Or that this is the end,
But this is a point at
Which to begin,
Because you have always
Had recovery within.

P.Bodi

If you've never met
Those who affirm,
Those who meet
You where you are,
Those whose love is
Unconditional and
Accepting,

Keep reaching out,
And you will find
That true connection.

The Hours In Between

A relationship that may have
Been positive once may not
Always be so, sometimes
There are people we
Simply outgrow.

P.Bodi

When you feel like things aren't changing,
When things feel still and stuck and wrong,
Even there that is a part of your growth,
It's been a part of your healing all along.

The Hours In Between

Maybe you're a stranger
To yourself, maybe you
Don't know who you are,
Maybe you've never asked
Yourself what you truly
Want for this life,

But you have time—
Time to uncover yourself,
To find what's true,
To fall in love with your
Own light.

Fall in love with your own light. You deserve that from yourself. You may be a stranger to yourself, but you are not strange. There is time to get to know yourself better, to know this life you want to live better. Connect back to what is true, to what is essentially you.

There are those we meet along our way,
Happy surprises—we find ourselves seen,
Those that help us become more whole,
Those who accept us in all that we are
And in all that we've been.

There is a life to be lived,
Only ever the way that you
Can live it,

You are endlessly worthy,
There are things to this
World that only you can
Bring, only you can give it.

The Hours In Between

There are many ways
To live a life, to make
Meaning unique to you,

It has endless value,
That which only you can do.

P.Bodi

How to define ourselves,
How to see our strengths,
How to be proud?

Thinking of all the ways
We 'should' be, our faults
And flaws so loud,

You deserve to see yourself
As you are, in multitudes,
In your many faces and words
And ways of existing,

There is endless beauty in
What makes you yourself,
In your simply being,
In the bravery that
Comes with living.

The Hours In Between

Hold onto it—
That which gives
You hope to carry
Onward, that light
That eases shame,

We all move into
Recovery in our
Own time, in
Our own way.

Your recovery is yours, no one else's.
How it looks and how it feels is unique to
your own journey.

We all have our own motivations to get better, to become more ourselves. Do not feel shame for the time it takes to heal, instead be proud that you are fighting for you—that you are putting energy towards your own growth. Hold onto what gives you hope, that will carry you forward into lasting and profound change.

The Hours In Between

This moment is a moment
Of growing, and change
Never slowing, closing to what
Has passed and opening to what
Is approaching,

And here you are, held
In a current always flowing,
Here you are becoming,
Dreaming, and hoping.

P.Bodi

This life is not a performance,
This life is not a show,
There is value in simply being,
In simply being known.

We tend to seek out that which
Confirms what we already
Believe; what if you
Learned to believe you
Were worthy of every
Good thing to come your
Way?

If you cultivated kindness,
If you didn't listen to shame?

P.Bodi

Bravery does not look
The same on everyone,
We all face that which
We are afraid of in the
Way that feels right
In the moment,

Even in moments of
Fear, of retreat, even
There you are growing.

The Hours In Between

Here we are,
In the middle of it all,
In however your middle
Arrives,

Be forever proud of the courage
It takes to live a life.

Here we are. At the cusp of the next moment, and then the next, and then the next after that. And sometimes, we can feel stuck. We may try and stand still against the current of change, but change is inevitable. So lean in. There is life to be found on the other side of resistance. Freedom is a falling away of the barriers we have set up in the hope that they will protect us, when all they have done is hold us back. Your story isn't over yet, and you are strong just for being here now.

The Hours In Between

You are lovable, despite how
Others may have hurt you when
You needed their acceptance and
Care most of all,

You deserved better, you *deserve*
Better, and being made to question
Your lovability is not your fault,

It's scary to open ourselves to being
Loved again, but we have to remind
Ourselves we are worth being loved
Unconditionally, that we are enough.

Familiar but unwelcome,
We let it take up space
That it does not deserve,
The negative thoughts that
Are hard to unlearn,

But you can speak a new
Narrative, tend to a kinder
Voice, question that which
Has given hurt, clarity gives
Us choice.

Mindset is the connector
Between what is external
And what is within,

Our reactions, our responses,
The ways that we come to live,

This can be shifted kinder,
Softer, calmer, true,
A healthier way to be,
A happier you.

P.Bodi

What you can't know:

That you'll never get better,
That you'll never find happiness,
That you'll never find meaning,

These thoughts cannot tell
The future, there is still
Hope to believe in,

Hold it a little closer than
Those familiar voices
Made of fear, because
You can still grow as
Long as you are here.

The Hours In Between

Your life matters,
To live is enough,
To be here at all
Is precious on
Its own,

And even if you don't
Know it yet, there is always
Warmth to be felt,
There is always
Light to grow.

P.Bodi

Your life is precious. You are in the flower that grows in the sun's light, and in the sun that gives the flower the warmth to thrive. You are no small thing. To be here now is a rare thing, you are rare, and you deserve to be here and to live a life you can call yours. Living is enough. You matter, and this living matters.

The Hours In Between

Let your heart beat loud,
Even when it is broken,
Even when you have wanted
It absent and silent,

You are a gift to this world,
Even on gray days you
Are a bright thing, you
Are glowing vibrant.

P.Bodi

We come into our lives
Knowing nothing, learning
From those around us,
And maybe you've been taught
That you are unworthy,
Unlovable, unimportant,

But they have taught you wrong.

You've been valuable, worthy,
Brilliant all along,

Always deserving, always
Worth supporting.

The Hours In Between

Decisions can be made and unmade,
The course can be shifted, you do not
Need to continue to commit to what
Is no longer right for you and your
Life at this moment or the next,

Situations change, you and your
Desires and priorities change,
We can always decide where
We will go, step by step.

You are the author of your life, and
We are the stories we choose to tell,
What is the narrative you will follow,
Given the challenges you've been dealt?

We can only control our own words,
Our own actions, the rest is in our
Interpretations and our reactions,

Your next chapter waits ahead of
You, so think on what you'll create,
There is the rest of your life to
Step into, there is a life just
For you to make.

The Hours In Between

When we question our worth,
We have become fixated on
What we have and do not have,
What we have done and have
Not done, and worst of all—
How we compare to others,

But life is not a game, there's
No tally keeping score,
There's no winning numbers,

Untangle yourself from the
Anxiety around achieving in
Order to feel worthy or validated,

Your worth as a human is innate,
Irrefutable, it cannot be
Measured or graded.

Your life is not a game to be won. Comparisons with others do not decide your worth. You are enough, and that has never been contingent on what you have achieved. Know that you deserve to be proud of being here now, no matter what you have done
or not done.

Your worth cannot be measured or graded, it simply is.

The Hours In Between

Productivity can become tied
To our worth, our value
Defined by achieving, by
Doing, felt externally instead
Of as an innate truth,

But you've always been worthy
And deserving, it's never been
Something you've needed to prove.

P.Bodi

You are capable,
Competent, maybe more
Than you believe,

What would you do,
What would you say,
If fear did not take
The lead?

We are not just our body,
And yet it is a part of us still—
Coming to love ourselves
Comes with loving this too,

To accept what is yours, the
Way that no one else is, that
Which is essentially you.

P.Bodi

There can come brambles
In our attempts to thrive,
And thorns and weeds too,
And even then, even here,
There is always a way through,

Your life is your own,
You choose the seeds
That you will tend to grow,
To flourish is something
You can come to know.

The Hours In Between

I have known what it is to contort
Myself into a person I am not,
A body bent into a
Shape it couldn't bear,
A mouth made to speak
Words that weren't mine,
But a stranger's, yes,
I have found myself strange.

But we've never never needed
To force this harmful type of change.

The most beautiful thing to me is
Letting yourself be, to accept who
You are in precisely how you are
At your most 'you', to step fully
Into yourself, to be honest, to be true.

P.Bodi

We can attempt to change parts of ourselves not out of a desire to be our most authentic selves, but instead to avoid judegment. We force a harmful sort of change that is driven by fear. To become who we think is deserving of love, more so than who we really are. That we are not enough as we are. To speak words that aren't ours, to act in a way unlike our true selves. But we do not need to put on a character. We can, if only little by little, step more fully into who we really are.

You are worth loving as yourself, you have always been enough simply for being you.

The Hours In Between

Loss changes how
We exist, how we
Live and respond,

Your feelings and
Your grief is natural,
Never something wrong,

This process can't be
Hurried, take all the time you
Need to heal, this hurt is
Necessary to feel.

You deserve to be heard,
To tell your story in your joy,
And in your pain the same,

To be seen fully, as a whole,
Without judgement or shame.

The Hours In Between

We can come to crave validation
From others when we feel we
Are not worthy on our own,

But no one can grant you
Self-love, it is a kindness
Only you can grow.

P.Bodi

Resting is not lazy
Or selfish or wrong,
We all need to slow
Down at times, to reflect,
To check-in with ourselves
Before we continue
And carry on.

The Hours In Between

Mental illness is not your
Fault, you didn't choose
To struggle, you are
Not to blame,

Don't let others tell
You otherwise, this
Does not deserve
Your shame.

Mental illness is not a personal failing, it is not a choice, and it has never deserved judgement or shame. No one is to blame for their struggle with mental health. You have always been deserving of empathy, kindness, understanding, and compassion. There is healing, recovery, and hope to be held. Shame has never helped anyone to become well. Remember that you are worth fighting for, and that you are worth supporting. This is your life to live, and your recovery is unique to you.

The Hours In Between

Loss is a rock thrown to
Water's calm surface,
Making ripples through
Everything that we are,
And everything that we've been,

Give yourself compassion, empathy, grace,
Give yourself time and space to heal,
Give yourself exactly what you need.

Care.

Care about your life.
Care about yourself.
Care about your future
And your potential for
Growth and healing.

Even if you don't care now,
Know that you have purpose,
Inherent, know that your
Life has meaning.

The Hours In Between

No one is quite like you,
Our differences are valuable,
We are separate but together
We are whole,

Treasure that which makes you unique,
And appreciate others in this too,
We are all part of the same story,
We each have a part to be told.

P.Bodi

We can fear our reflections,
Because what do we see?
Is it someone you don't
Like? Someone you don't
Want to be?

But know this to be true:
You will only ever have you,
And you are beautiful and
Enough as you came into
This being, onto this earth,

Never have you needed
To question your worth.

The Hours In Between

We can be proud of others
Without comparison or jealousy,
There is room for all of us,
Your peers are not the enemy.

Jealousy is the ashamed and blinding fear that drags us all down. That is certain of scarcity, of there not being enough room for all of us. It turns our peers into the enemy while turning us into someone concerned too much with ourselves and not concerned enough about our surroundings as a balanced whole. Because there is enough room for all of our unique gifts and strengths. Being proud of someone else does not make you less-than. It does not make you worthless. Let others lift you up, and lift them up too.

The Hours In Between

You are not wrong for having feelings.
Strong feelings, difficult feelings,
Like an open wound you
Can't ignore,

You are not too much,
Be compassionate to yourself
And your struggle, there is healing
To be had, hope and coping skills
To be yours.

This is natural,

This hurting,
This unflinching pain,
These wounds that
Come with living
A life,

It is normal to be upset,
It is normal to feel fear
And sadness, it is
Normal to cry.

The Hours In Between

Why do we do the things we
Do? Why, these habits.
Why, these routines?

Pause.

Reflect, gentle, is this the
Future you had dreamed?

If you have been living a
Life away from yourself,
Apart from the truest
Version of you,

What, now, can you
Shift only a little? What,
Now, can you improve?

We can end up living a life unaligned. Not always in large ways, but small ways too. Habits we've picked up along the way, routines and ruts that we don't even realize we have fallen into. This can be your moment of clarity. It's not a call to change your whole life, or to regret the way you've been living. Instead, to turn towards what you want for yourself at your best. We can make subtle shifts that turn into great change over time. Notice what has become habit. Become aware when routine becomes negative. And in turn, become more you.

The Hours In Between

If you've been told that
You're not enough, that
You're not worthy, if you've
Been told that the life
You've lived falls short,

Know that this life is
Not another's to live,
But only ever yours,

You are enough as you are,
You are deserving of love
And of compassion,
No matter what you've
Achieved or haven't.

You are not others' expectations of you. You are not of their purpose, or of their ideals, or of their desires. Your life has only ever been yours. You are worthy, you are enough, and you are deserving of being and becoming exactly who you want to be, no matter the thoughts of others. Your achievements and what you haven't done—these are external. These cannot prove or disprove your worth. Your worth is unwavering, true.
It has never been tied to what
you do or don't do.

The Hours In Between

Find comfort in what you can,
Life has a way of stripping us
Down to parts, to feel less
Whole, less of ourselves,

Anchor yourself, strong, to
What makes you feel like
The truest version of yourself.

Your life matters,
You are a rarity
Given shape,

You bring light to
This being in the way
No one else can,
There is magic
Only you can make.

The flowers do not compare,
No competition to be had,
The sun's light is theirs to share,

We can learn to live the same,
Embracing our own beauty,
Embracing our own selves
As we come, learning the
Gentle art of self-love.

P.Bodi

You are competent
And brave beyond
What you may believe,

You are what you seek,
You are what you need.

The Hours In Between

Maybe you've wished
To blend into walls,
To not be seen so
As not to be hurt,

But there are those
Who want to know
All of you, those who
Will help you know
Your worth.

P.Bodi

I see you, those who are afraid of being seen. Because I have been you; I know what it is to keep myself quiet, to keep myself small. But your voice deserves to be heard. You are worthy of taking up space, you can be proud, and the world needs your light. Let yourself be seen, let yourself be bright.

Let yourself be honest,
Authentic, true,

You deserve to be
Known as you.

P.Bodi

I have known what
Felt like dead-ends,
Walls on all sides with
Nowhere else to turn,

And now, this is what I have learned:

If you're alive, there is still
Endless room to grow, I wish
I could've told myself then,

This pain is not all you'll know.

The Hours In Between

Shame is of silence, buried deep,
The secrets we feel we need
To keep, because what will
Others say?

But there are those who want
To know all of you, to be there
For you, to hear you, those who
Will challenge that shame.

P.Bodi

We come across people in our lives that see us exactly how we are—with flaws, worries, beauty and strength, and decide to be there for it all. To want to hear it all, that which you have felt you needed to be silent about. You are worth that unconditional kind of empathy and love. The kind that wants the best for you, the kind that sees your best.

The Hours In Between

Productivity need
Not validate your worth,
Accolades and achievements
Are something to be proud of,
But you have been enough
From the beginning,

Your value is inherent
No matter the manner
Of how you're living.

Your value is inherent. We are born to this life worthy. You have never needed to prove this to others or to yourself. Be proud of what you achieve while you are here, and continue to grow, but this life is not for show.

The Hours In Between

We are not outsiders,
We are not on the edges
Of what it means to be
A person,

We are just as lovable
As anyone else, we are
Just as deserving.

We often feel that we are outside of the bounds of what it means to be human, what it means to be worthy. Even that we are less than human; an outsider to life itself.

But your lovability is no less than anyone else. Your value is undeniable, and you are endlessly deserving of kindness, connection, empathy, and understanding.

The Hours In Between

What calls you to rise,
That mirrors the sun?
What fervent light
Beats in your chest,
That speaks:

"No, I'm nowhere
Near done."

P.Bodi

If you've ever been a worrier,
If the future has been a big
Scary question mark, if you've
Thought of the next year
Not with excitement but
With fear,

You are not a alone,
Life is full of unknowns,
And still we can grow,

We can face what comes,
We can learn to take change
As it arrives, even from our
Darkest days we can thrive.

The Hours In Between

Fear need not be a barrier,
But instead, a guide we
Can follow, fast heartbeat
Leading the way ahead,

Fear can tell us what we
Need to do next, it can
Be a beacon instead.

Let fear be a beacon, not a barrier. A guide, not a guard. Fear can tell us what to do next, where to go next; what will bring us growth. Change is on the other side of terror. They are joined, essentially so. Facing our fears is how we become greater. Small, quiet life in the shadow of what we could be, in the shadow of a fear we feel we cannot overcome, is only ever worse than the fear itself.

Draw on strength, on support. It does not need to be done alone. And you are more competent, more brave, more ready than you may believe.

The Hours In Between

I can't promise it will get better,
I can't promise myself I'll always
Feel well, because life ebbs and
Flows and falls and rises and
Only time will tell,

And all that you can do,
Is do your best for you,

You have always been deserving,
You have always been worth the fight,
And even with all that is yet to be
I think we'll be alright.

P.Bodi

It is a kindness to be here now,
To have stayed, to still try,
To be able to bring light
To this world and to see
It the same,

There is purpose in you,
There is more to you
Than pain.

The Hours In Between

Love who you have been,
Even in your hardest moments,
Give empathy, give your past
Your compassion, this love is
Healing, this love is lasting.

P.Bodi

Not one of us knows what
The future will bring,
Only that we will
Have ourselves,

You have strength within
You just for being here now,
And it is brave to know
When to ask for help.

To feel could never be wrong,
Even the hard emotions have value,
They have meaning,

Every day is worth living in,
There is hope here,
There is healing.

It is a beautiful thing to be able to feel. Sensitivity can be a strength. It lends empathy, it creates connection, and it gives you more insight into the human experience. This is valuable. We may see the painful things and the negative feelings as a burden, but I have come to believe even the hard days are worth living in.

The Hours In Between

You don't need to
Have all the answers,
There is strength built
In the learning, in the
Making mistakes and
Growing from them,
And no one knows it all,

It is human to rise,
And it is human to fall.

P.Bodi

Your pain is not less
For someone else having
It 'worse',

Be kind to yourself
Always, we cannot
Measure hurt.

The Hours In Between

Warmth we come to feel,
And warmth we've never known,
Maybe love is a kindness that
You've never been shown,

This is a tragedy,
And your hurt is significant,
You are deserving as we all are,
Your worth has never been different,

Love is not impossible,
Meet others as you are in the
Way that you've been living,

Find those who will accept
You here and now, those
Whose love for you is a given.

P.Bodi

Relapse does not mean you
Have lost what you have
Learned in recovery,

We become stronger each
Time we get back up, with
Every new discovery.

The Hours In Between

I know what it is to want
To leave, to see life as
Only pain instead
Of purpose,

We all have it in us,
We all have that seed
That seeks the light,
That has only ever
Wanted to flourish.

It is in you, even in your lowest moments. That seed that seeks the light, that has only ever wanted to flourish. Despite what you may be feeling on your darkest days, there is hope in you to be nurtured and grown. Your pain is real, and so is your strength.

The Hours In Between

Sometimes change is quiet,
Subtle shifts that surmount
Into transformation,

So remind yourself of
How far you've come,
Be proud of the person
You have been and
Who you have become.

P.Bodi

All little travellers,
With no map, or
'X' marks the spot,

We keep on walking,
Stepping forward
With all that
We've got,

Let burn the wick
That sheds the dark,
To let live your light,

Because there you
Are, there we are,
Glowing steady,
Bright.

The Hours In Between

You are not a conclusion,
Each second brings
You a new beginning,
Change is inevitable,
And this is you doing
Your best, this is living.

P.Bodi

You are in every day that
Has passed in your being,
In you is held the sun's light,
That star burning bright,
Here, right now as
You're breathing,

Warmth is you,
Radiant, shining,
You are morning,
You are dawn's
Soft rising.

The Hours In Between

We hold onto regret
As if it can change
Our future, as if
Shame can heal
Our hurt,

Know that today is
Today and yesterday
Has passed and is done,
We can both learn from
Our mistakes, and
Be proud of how far
We've come.

Regret is that heavy weight that chains us to our shame, to a past that cannot be undone. Thoughts fixed on a time that cannot be changed. But we have today. We have tomorrow. Shame cannot heal, but learning can. Reflection can. Stepping forward into ourselves and into our own self-compassion and self-forgiveness can. Today is today, and there's no better place to grow from.

The Hours In Between

See how the clouds attempt
To obscure sun's light,
Yet still it shines behind
Cover and storm, it still
Glows stunning and bright,

Hope is just the same,
Waiting, patient and present
To rise beyond the night.

P.Bodi

You being here now
Is a gift to those around,
You are a gift,

You are enough,
And your absence
Would be felt,
Your brilliance
Would be missed.

The Hours In Between

Do not fault yourself
For that which it has
Taken you to survive—

Because here you are,
Doing the best that
You can, here you
Are alive.

P.Bodi

It is in the waiting,
It is in patience,
The kindness we
Gift to a self standing
Up ahead,

We will do our best
For ourselves, we will
Look back and be grateful
That our story didn't end.

The Hours In Between

Let go of the day
When it is done,
Let its weight fall
Off your shoulders,

Tomorrow waits,
Your story isn't over.

When the day is edging into dusk, and then into night, and then into tomorrow, know that while you cannot change what has passed, you can release what has come and gone, you can let the thoughts around it, the anxieties, the fear, go free. We can move forward without the weight of yesterday pulling our attention and energy backwards. You are here in this moment, and in no other. Give your full attention to now. Breathe and breathe and breathe. Tomorrow waits, and your story isn't over yet.

The Hours In Between

There is a self you
Haven't met just yet,
Waiting beyond the horizon,
Waiting for you patient and bright,

That future self is worth the fight.

P.Bodi

There are those we meet
In life that we never
Want to let go,

Those that feel essential,
Those that feel like home,

Maybe you haven't found
Them yet, maybe they are
Waiting, patient to be met.

The Hours In Between

Every day you've lived—
The hard, the painful,
And the happy ones too,

They are all worthy of
Being felt by you.

P.Bodi

Recovery is not a simple thing,
Not a smooth line upwards
From illness to wellness
Lasting forever,

Even relapse, even struggle
And pain and hopelessness
Are found on the journey
To getting better.

The Hours In Between

Every day brings with it
New growth, so choose
To live in beautiful change,

You will look back,
Grateful for your courage,
Proud of who you became.

Live in beautiful change. Embrace what is growing around you and within you. Each new day is a new world to be explored, and a new you to become. Think of yourself standing somewhere up ahead, looking back at you now. Know that you will be grateful for the courage it takes to keep moving forward. Know that you will be endlessly proud.

We are all walking into the dark,
Little embers, sparks of light
Into what is the unknown,

Stoke the fire,
Fan the flames,
Let yourself do what
You've always been
Meant to do: let
Yourself shine, let
Yourself glow.

P.Bodi

You are a work in progress,
And what a beautiful thing to be,
Hold onto excitement for
What you're yet to see.

The Hours In Between

If the path ahead isn't clear,
Take comfort in what is human:
To explore, to taste, to challenge
Yourself in the trying, in the
Becoming more you,

In living more and more
In your truth.

P.Bodi

You have so much to be
Proud of, most of all for
Being here,

You are of strength,
You are of endless growth,
You are more than your fear.

Keep stepping
Into your
Next chapter,

There is more life
To be lived, your
Story matters.

P.Bodi

Try and try and
Don't stop when
You fall, when you
Make mistakes—
Know that this
Is human,

Life is for living,
Life is for growing,
Life is for always
Improving.

The Hours In Between

Growth is never ending,
Never done, never
Finished, not a
Race for you
To run,

Give compassion,
Give patience,
This moment is
A moment of
Becoming, not
Merely a moment
Of waiting.

This is not merely a moment of waiting. It is one of patience, compassion, of knowing that you are becoming more of yourself all of the time. Know that you are whole as you are, and at the same time, you are never done changing. There is no end-point at which we can say we are done with our growth; it is a process that carries us forward. Take comfort in this, that we are always becoming a better version of ourselves. That we are beautiful works in progress.

The Hours In Between

Maybe you don't
Believe it yet,
Maybe you don't
Know how it feels,

But you have it in
You to hope, you have
It in you to heal.

P.Bodi

Living a life takes courage,
Be proud that you met today,
That you've lived through
What difficulties you've had to face,
That still you've decided to stay.

The Hours In Between

Receive the world
As it is, as dark days
Come and as the light
Ones lift us like the sun
Risen from the night,

Your life has always
Been worth the fight.

P.Bodi

You don't have to know what to say,
You don't always have to know
What to do, just keep stepping
Forward into you.

The Hours In Between

I hope you stay,
Learn what it is
To live the life
You were meant
To live, to find
Purpose and
Joy and connection,

There is a place for all
Of us here, you are not
The exception.

P.Bodi

You are of stunning light,
A life worth being known,
So live proudly, blossom
Into your own.

The Hours In Between

If only there were a path to follow,
With the end beautiful and known,
Yet nothing is ever sure or certain,
Not when we step forward as
Ourselves and on our own,

Hold space for what good can
Come of your efforts to grow,
In this—this becoming,
This making of a home.

P.Bodi

This making of a home is not without fear. Fear is a natural companion to the unknown. Change carries us forward even when we resist that questioning dark. The path is not lit. Tomorrow does not always go as planned. The end is never known, and yet beauty can still come to us in the small, in the great, in the painful, and in the fulfilling. Hold space for all that comes, for all that you become, and for all that you learn of your life and of yourself.

The Hours In Between

I have been gifted hope
When I had none,
Those around held
It for me for a time,
Until I could call
It mine,

If hope is quiet for you now,
Let me do the same as they
Did for me, let me hold that
Hope for you, until it is a
Truth that you believe.

These are the hours in-between who you are and who you will be. Like a flower blooming into day, receive the sun's light and warmth, open to beautiful change, and flourish into your own.

If these poems have helped you feel seen, heard, understood, or have provided a sense of hope, you can find more of my writing on Instagram @p.bodii

Let this collection be a reminder of your strength, of your capacity for growth and change, and of the bright hope that has always been yours to hold.

Printed in Great Britain
by Amazon